How To Form A Texas LLC

A Quick Legal Guide

SECOND EDITION

By Mike Young, Esq.

Copyright Notice

Table of Contents

How To Use This Guide

Each Quick Legal Guide™ is designed as a resource to quickly learn the most important things you need to know about one business legal topic.

In the *Introduction* section, we'll reveal three key advantages of setting up a Texas limited liability company.

In *Chapter 1*, we'll discuss steps you'll want to take before setting up your LLC.

Then we'll show you how to file the formation paperwork with the State of Texas in *Chapter 2*.

In *Chapter 3*, we'll cover important federal and state tax issues for your LLC.

What to include in your LLC's operating agreement (and why you need such an agreement) is discussed in *Chapter 4*.

And in *Chapter 5*, we'll cover setting up your LLC's bank account(s) the right way.

Chapter 6 reveals four common types of business insurance you'll want to consider for your company.

Finally, *Chapter 7* identifies 10 key issues you should address in your company's employment agreements.

There's also a *Quick Start Checklist* so you know what to do after reading this guide.

Additional material, including a *Resources* section, is located at the back of this guide. These reference materials should be used as-needed but aren't essential to understanding the topic.

Introduction - Why Set Up a Texas Limited Liability Company?

The three primary reasons for forming a for-profit Texas LLC to do business are:

(1) personal liability protection;
(2) paperwork reduction; and
(3) low taxes.

1. Liability Protection

A Texas limited liability company offers substantially the same personal liability protections as a Texas corporation does. If you observe a few legal formalities, your personal assets (home, vehicles, personal bank accounts, etc.) are protected if your company gets sued. This means that if everything goes to Hell in a handbasket, you still should be able to walk away with what you've made even if the business is sued into bankruptcy.

Example: While speeding, your employee kills someone in a head-on collision while driving one of your LLC's vehicles. To the extent automobile insurance doesn't cover the wrongful death claims, the decedent's family will probably be limited to going after the LLC's assets but won't be able to touch your personal assets to satisfy any judgment obtained.

There are three major *exceptions* to this personal liability protection:

(a) not observing legal formalities;
(b) taxes; and
(c) environmental claims.

These exceptions exist *both* for LLCs and corporations.

Legal Formalities Example: You decide to ignore the existence of the LLC as a separate entity and treat company bank accounts and other business assets as your own personal assets.
Taxes Example: When taxes are due, your LLC doesn't pay them to the government.
Environmental Claims Example: Your company dumps toxic waste into a river.

In each of these examples, there's a good chance you'll be personally on the hook to the extent your LLC doesn't have the assets or insurance to handle the claims.

2. Less Paperwork

Running a Texas LLC is a piece of cake compared to a corporation. Your LLC's governing legal document is an operating agreement (similar to a corporation's shareholder agreement and corporate bylaws). However, unlike a corporation, a limited liability company doesn't have time wasted with Board of Directors meetings, shareholders meetings, meeting minutes, issuance and transfer of stock certificates, endless votes, unanimous consents, etc.

You'll likely find it takes about 1/10th the time and legal paperwork to maintain an LLC as it does a corporation.

3. Low Taxes

The State of Texas is well known for being business-friendly. Unlike most other states, Texas owns the mineral rights on public lands and uses oil and gas leases to partially finance government. This is one of the main reasons why Texas has no personal state income tax (a benefit that's attractive to employers and employees alike) and low business taxes.

Because Texas also has a low franchise tax, most LLCs don't have to pay this tax until they start making a lot of money.

Like most states, Texas *does* have a sales tax on many products. It will be collected from retail customers at point of sale and remitted by the LLC to the State Comptroller's office. Many LLC owners do this without help. Some have a bookkeeper or accountant handle the paperwork instead.

Chapter 1 - Before You Set Up Your Texas LLC

It's a lot easier to get your Texas limited liability company up and running correctly if you take some preliminary steps before the entity is formed. These include:

1. Asset identification;
2. Determination of ownership interests;
3. Picking possible names for your LLC;
4. Decide how the LLC will be managed;
5. Select a registered agent; and
6. Choose your company's mailing address.

Here's how to handle each of these six tasks...

1. Identify LLC Assets

First, you'll want to identify the assets you'll be transferring to the business entity including capital contributions. If you have an existing business, such as a sole proprietorship, this list can be a long one. On the other hand, if your LLC is a startup venture, chances are your list will have 10-20 assets you're planning to transfer into the entity once it is formed.

2. Ownership

You need to decide who will own the business. Just as a corporation is owned by its shareholders, a Texas LLC is owned by its members. You'll need to identify who the members are going to be and what percentage of ownership each member will have.

Just because someone is helping you with the business doesn't mean they should own equity in your LLC. There are many ways to compensate someone for what they bring to the table without handing over equity to them. For example, you may want to share a percentage of profits, offer performance bonuses, etc.

That being said, don't forget people who should own equity. It's fairly common for a married couple to decide to form a LLC to replace the informal partnership they've had for a business they own. However, the spouse who approaches the attorney forgets about the marriage when it comes to identifying who should own equity in the LLC. Don't end up in divorce court because equity ownership of your business was mishandled.

3. Names

Even if you have an existing business that operates under a name, you'll want to use Internet search engines (Google, Bing etc.) to research 3 to 5 potential names for your Texas LLC (be sure to add "LLC" to the end of each name). Find something that's relatively unique that doesn't infringe upon an existing trademark or service mark. Be sure to perform a free trademark search at the U.S. Patent & Trademark Office's website (see *Resources* section at the end of this guide) to ensure your potential LLC names don't infringe on federally registered marks.

Rank these 3 to 5 potential LLC names in order of priority. This is the list that your business attorney will work from when filing the paperwork to form your LLC. As part of filing, name searches of Texas business entities will be performed, and any potential names that are too similar to an existing Texas company will be tossed in favor of one that's more likely to be approved by the government.

Example: If your top name choice is "ABC Plumbing LLC" and there's already a Texas corporation named "ABCD Plumbing Inc.," there's a good chance the filing paperwork will be rejected and you will have to use another name that's not similar to an existing Texas business entity.

4. Management

You need to decide ahead of time how your company will be managed. Will you have a separate manager or will the owners (members) manage the company?

In most cases, it makes sense to have the LLC managed by its members. Having a separate manager sometimes occurs in situations where there is one person actively running the business but there are passive investors in the business who will own equity but will not be involved managing the limited liability company.

5. Registered Agent

Your LLC will need a registered agent that can, among other things, accept service of process during business hours if your company is sued. Note that this must be a physical address, not a post office (PO) box or private mailbox (PMB).

Although an LLC's member can serve as registered agent, as a practical matter it makes a lot of sense (for privacy and other reasons) to use a commercial registered agent service to handle this for your LLC.

In the *Resources* section at the back of this guide, I provide you with the name and contact information for the registered agent that I and many law firm clients use for our Texas LLCs. In just a few minutes online, you can set up a registered agent for your LLC even before it is formed.

There's a chicken-and-egg dilemma when forming a Texas LLC when using a commercial registered agent service. The government wants you to identify the registered agent for your LLC in the formation paperwork but you don't know yet whether the government will approve the top name you have selected for your proposed entity.

Here's how to handle the issue. Set up the registered agent using the name of the top pick for your LLC even if you don't know whether it will be approved. If approved by the Texas government, you're good to go. If you have to use a different name for your LLC in order to get it approved, just let your registered agent know right after the entity is formed so that agent can update its paperwork to reflect the real name of your limited liability company.

6. Business Address

You should decide in advance the business mailing address you will be using for your entity. For personal privacy and safety, this address should not be your home address.

If your company already has a physical location outside your home, you can use that location for your business address. However, if your business is home-based, you should consider renting a private mailbox (PMB) for your LLC's mailing address.

Note that a PMB is not a post office (PO) box. PO boxes are rented at U.S. Postal Service facilities. In contrast, a PMB is rented from a private business entity such as a UPS Store, Mr. Parcel, PostNet, and the like.

Why choose a PMB instead of a PO Box? As part of the private sector, PMBs tend to provide better service, longer business hours, and more privacy than using a PO Box. This is particularly helpful when receiving packages.

Chapter 2 - Filing The Formation Paperwork

Texas Secretary of State

You'll file the paperwork to form your limited liability company with the Texas Secretary of State's office. Although paper filings are accepted (not recommended), as a practical matter it's quicker and easier to file electronically via the Internet using SOSDirect, the Secretary's online business service.

If you decide to file offline using real paper, you can find forms to download at the Secretary of State's website too. (See *Resources* section at the end of this guide).

Whether filed offline or electronically, you'll be setting up your Texas LLC by filing a *Certificate of Formation*. If you use the *SOSDirect* online system, you will fill out a few pages of forms that will generate this certificate for you.

Fees

The filing fee is currently $300.[1] There is a 2.7% convenience fee for paying by credit card, which you should expect to pay if you're filing electronically via SOSDirect.

If you're filing offline, you can pay by check, money order, or credit card. You may also pay with cash if you file in person at the Secretary of State's office in Austin, Texas.

SOS Approval

If you file online using SOSDirect, you should expect a decision from the Secretary of State's office within 1 to 2 business days. If your LLC is approved, you'll receive a download link for a compressed zip file that contains your LLC's formation documents. This will include Adobe Acrobat PDF format copies of your Certificate of Formation, a Certificate of Filing that shows your Certificate of Formation has been filed, and a letter from the Secretary of State's office that explains a few things about your LLC.

---

[1] At the time this chapter was updated in February 2019. Fees may change.

If you file *electronically* but don't receive an email response from the Secretary of State's office within 5 to 7 business days, be sure to check the spam folder in your email account to see if the response was inadvertently placed there before you call the Secretary's office to follow up on your filing status.

If you file *offline*, it will typically take longer and you will receive your approval information by snail mail.

SOS Denial

If you file online using *SOSDirect*, but the Secretary of State's office denies your filing, you should expect to receive an email with this decision within 1 to 2 business days. If your LLC filing is denied, you'll receive a download link for a compressed zip file that contains a PDF file that explains why the Secretary of State denied it.

The primary reason for such a denial is the proposed name of your LLC is too similar to the name of an existing Texas limited liability company or corporation. For example, if the first two words of the proposed name are identical to those of another Texas entity, the name will likely be rejected.

If you think the decision was wrong, you can ask that it be reconsidered by stating your reasons why the filing should be accepted. This works *sometimes*.

The usual solution is to correct the issue that led to the denial (e.g. use a different name for your LLC) and re-file.

Of course, if you filed offline, it will typically take longer for you to receive the denial information by snail mail. This is another reason why it is beneficial to use the online system instead to speed up the formation of your LLC.

Chapter 3 - LLC Taxes

Federal Taxes

There are two things you will want to do for your new Texas LLC with regard to the U.S. Internal Revenue Service (IRS):

1. Get an Employer Identification Number; and
2. Decide how you want the IRS to treat your LLC for income tax purposes.

Throughout this chapter, there will be references to IRS forms. In the *Resources* section at the end of this guide, you'll find links to these forms and to the page where you can apply online for an Employer Identification Number.

1. Employer Identification Number

First, get an Employer Identification Number (EIN) for your LLC. You will use that EIN when setting up your LLC's bank account and for dealing with others in business transactions where your LLC's taxpayer identification number is needed (e.g. IRS Form W-9).

2. Tax Treatment Decision

Second, you need to make a decision on how you want your LLC to be treated for federal income tax purposes.

Most entrepreneurs choose to have the LLC treated as a pass-through entity. For a single member Texas LLC, the limited liability company is treated as a "disregarded entity" and the income passes through to the member as if the LLC was a sole proprietorship. Your income gets reported on a schedule (Schedule C) attached to your annual personal income tax return (IRS Form 1040).

If the LLC has more than one member, it can also be a pass-through entity where the LLC is treated as a partnership with the income passing through to each member as if they were partners. The LLC files a partnership tax return and each member receives a Schedule K-1 (IRS Form 1065) showing the member's share of the LLC's income.

To have your LLC treated as a pass-through entity, you file nothing with the IRS. That's the default status for tax treatment.

However, a few LLCs elect to be treated as a Subchapter S corporation for income tax purposes. This requires filing an election for such treatment with the IRS. Otherwise, the entity will be treated as a pass-through entity. The primary reason for electing Subchapter S tax treatment is when there is a way to legally minimize taxes by paying a salary to one or more LLC members while having the rest of the income treated as capital gains.

State Taxes

Although there is no Texas state personal income tax, the Texas Comptroller of Public Accounts is important because of franchise taxes and sales taxes.

If you are selling retail products in Texas, your LLC will collect a sales tax from Texas customers (presently 8.25% in most parts of the state[2]) and remit to the state's Comptroller. This means your LLC will first need to apply for a sales tax permit. See *Resources* section.

---

[2] At the time this chapter was updated in February 2019. Rates may change.

The Texas franchise tax is imposed on business entities' revenue for the privilege of doing business within the state. It's important to note that many LLCs do not owe the tax because they don't earn enough to hit the threshold to pay the tax. However, even if no franchise tax is owed, you still must file franchise tax reports to show you don't owe the tax.

Chapter 4 - Texas LLC Operating Agreement

Your LLC operating agreement is a written contract between the LLC and its owners (members) that serves as a guide for how you will run your Texas limited liability company. Because it is a legally binding agreement that affects your rights, responsibilities, and potential liabilities, you'll want to have the contract prepared by a qualified business lawyer who understands Texas limited liability companies.

Key Provisions

Although the contents of your LLC's operating agreement will vary based upon your particular needs, here are some of the key areas covered in most agreements.

- The company's name and purpose
- Limitations on owner (member) liability
- How the LLC will be taxed (as a pass-through entity or as a corporation)
- How the LLC will keep its accounting guides (cash or accrual method)

- Capital contributions by members now and in the future
- Percentages of LLC ownership for each member
- How the LLC's profits are to be allocated to its members
- Who manages the LLC
- How equity can be transferred by a member to the LLC, other members, and third parties
- When is a member no longer a member
- How the LLC can be dissolved, wound up, and have its assets liquidated
- Copies of the LLC's Certificate of Formation and Certificate of Filing attached as exhibits to the agreement.

Copies of the Agreement

After your LLC agreement is properly signed, be sure to make copies and store the original in a safe place. You will want to take a copy of the signed agreement (with the LLC's certificates of filing and formation attached as exhibits) with you when you open a bank account. As a practical matter, the first use of an operating agreement for many start-up LLCs is to open your company bank accounts.

Chapter 5 - LLC Banking

As part of setting up your Texas limited liability company, you'll want to open at least one company bank account in the LLC's name rather than using your personal accounts. This is typically a business checking account, a savings account, and perhaps a merchant account for accepting credit card payments.

In addition to the funds (capital contributions) you'll be using to open the account(s), be sure to bring the following with you to the bank.

- All LLC members (and managers) who will be authorized to sign checks on the account(s).
- Government-issued photo ID (e.g. Texas driver's license or U.S. Passport) for each signatory
- A copy of your signed LLC operating agreement, including the LLC's certificates of formation and filing as exhibits
- Your LLC's Employer Identification Number (EIN) obtained from the IRS
- Evidence of business mailing address (varies by bank)

Each signatory may also want to bring their Social Security card with them in case the bank asks to see it. However, the LLC's EIN should be tied to the accounts, not a member or manager's Social Security Number.

If you're accepting payments online, you may also want to set up a PayPal account and tie it to one of your LLC's bank accounts.

Chapter 6 - Business Insurance

Liability Insurance

Although having an LLC will protect you from most personal liability claims if your business is sued, chances are you will want to continue running the business rather than having its assets sold off to satisfy any judgments obtain against it.

That's where business liability insurance plays an important role. Working with your financial advisor or business insurance broker, buy a general liability insurance policy that provides you with the amount of protection you need. If necessary, you may also want to obtain an umbrella liability policy and perhaps policy riders for specific risks in your type of business.

This isn't a guide about liability insurance. Just a reminder that such insurance does play a role in protecting you and your company no matter what type of Texas business entity (LLC, corporation, partnership, sole proprietorship, etc.) you have.

Can liability insurance replace the need for the protective shield that a Texas limited liability company provides? Not really. It's simply extra protection to help you if you need it.

Key Person Insurance

Sometimes referred to as "key man insurance," key person insurance is used to protect your LLC if one or more members is vital to running the company. If that vital member dies or becomes incapacitated, key person insurance kicks in to cover the losses incurred because of the death or disability.

A key person insurance policy is typically owned by the Texas limited liability company, the LLC is the policy beneficiary, and the policy is terminated when that important member is no longer important to the company (e.g. the person leaves the LLC to work elsewhere).

Is key person insurance necessary? Although it is not mandatory, such insurance is common when there is a multi-member LLC that depends upon one or two people to make the company successful. This is particularly true where members who are passive investors want to protect themselves in case an essential person running the company can no longer do so because of death or disability.

Property Insurance

If you own or rent property for your business, i.e. your LLC has a physical location rather than just a PMB or PO Box, you should consider getting property/renter's insurance to cover risk of loss in case something happens (e.g. fire, flood, theft, tornado, earthquake, etc.).

Auto Insurance

If your LLC owns or leases a vehicle, get appropriate auto insurance. Be sure the insurance policy covers all the people who will be driving the vehicle (e.g. members, employees, etc.).

Chapter 7 - Employment Agreements

If your LLC is going to have employees (e.g. a salaried manager), it may make sense to have your business lawyer create written contracts to protect your company.

Although the specifics of employment agreements vary, here are some key issues that are often covered in such contracts.

- Term of employment
- Compensation
- The employee's duties
- Paid time off
- Reimbursement of expenses
- Ownership of intellectual property rights
- Termination of employment
- Non-competition
- Confidentiality
- Dispute resolution

Quick Start Checklist

Here are five things to do to get your Texas limited liability company set up and running the right way.

_____ 1. Walk through the steps in *Chapter 1 - Before You Set Up Your Texas LLC.*

_____ 2. Have an experienced Texas business lawyer set up your LLC for you and prepare your LLC's operating agreement.

_____ 3. Take care of the federal and state tax issues identified in *Chapter 3.*

_____ 4. Open your LLC's bank account(s).

_____ 5. Meet with your insurance broker or agent to get the business insurance protection you need.

Do You Need Help With Your Texas LLC?

If you want help from a business lawyer to set up a new Texas LLC or get your legal paperwork in order for an existing Texas entity, let's talk about your legal needs.

Go to https://mikeyounglaw.com/appointments/ or call 214-546-4247 to schedule your phone consultation.

Just choose a day and time that's convenient and I'll call you.

Wishing you the best.

-Mike

Michael E. Young, J.D., LL.M.
Attorney & Counselor at Law

About The Author

Since 1994, Internet Lawyer Mike Young has helped business clients prevent and solve legal problems.

President of the Internet Attorneys Association LLC, Mike has a law office in Plano, Texas (a Dallas suburb), and also serves as a foreign legal consultant in the Republic of Panama.

Happily married, Mike enjoys spending time with his family, walking his dogs, and self-defense training.

To learn more, go to MikeYoungLaw.com. While there, be sure to subscribe to his complimentary newsletter where you will receive important business legal news and tips by email.

Rate and Review

If you have found this guide helpful, please post a positive customer review for it at Amazon.com.

Whether you liked the guide or not, please send me a copy of the review you submitted to Amazon because feedback is important for updates and writing new guides too.

Just email a copy to me at mike@mikeyounglaw.com and I promise to respond.

Thank you.

-Mike

Glossary

ACKNOWLEDGEMENT – A letter from the Texas Secretary of State that acknowledges your LLC is now formed and explains various issues about your new limited liability company.

CERTIFICATE OF FILING – A certificate issued by the Texas Secretary of State when approving your LLC's Certificate of Formation. If you filed electronically, a PDF copy of this certificate will be emailed to you.

CERTIFICATE OF FORMATION – The certificate that forms your Texas LLC. If you filed electronically, the Texas Secretary of State will email you a copy of the certificate with the Certificate of Filing once your LLC's formation is approved.

DISREGARDED ENTITY – A single member Texas limited liability company that is disregarded for income tax purposes by the IRS. The income passes through to the member as if the entity didn't exist and is taxed the same as a sole proprietorship.

DOMESTIC LLC – For purposes of this guide, a domestic LLC is a limited liability company formed in Texas. This contrasts with a foreign LLC that is formed in another state or country but may be doing business in Texas.

EIN – The Employer Identification Number issued to a Texas LLC by the IRS even if the limited liability company does not have any employees. The EIN is one type of IRS Taxpayer Identification Number (TIN).

FOREIGN LLC – For purposes of this guide, a foreign LLC is a limited liability company formed in a jurisdiction (another state or country) outside of Texas. This contrasts with a domestic LLC that is formed in Texas. A foreign LLC may qualify to do business in Texas.

FRANCHISE TAX – This state tax is imposed on Texas LLCs and other business entities for the privilege of doing business within the State of Texas. Many businesses do not earn enough to owe the tax. However, franchise tax reports must still be filed with the Texas Comptroller of Public Accounts showing no tax is due.

IRS – The U.S. Internal Revenue Service

KEY PERSON – A manager or member that your Texas LLC depends upon for the company's success. Key person insurance is often purchased to cover losses associated with this person's death or disability.

LIMITED LIABILITY CORPORATION – An inaccurate term frequently used by non-lawyers to describe a limited liability company. Although a corporation does have limited liability too, a limited liability company is a separate type of legal entity that is not a corporation.

MANAGER – A person who manages a Texas limited liability company. Most Texas LLCs do not appoint a separate manage but leave management to the LLC's owners (members).

MEMBER – A person or entity that owns equity in a Texas limited liability company. This is the equivalent of being a corporation's shareholder.

OPERATING AGREEMENT – A Texas LLC's operating agreement is a contract between the limited liability company's owners (members) that addresses how the LLC will be run and the respective rights and responsibilities of the members. The operating agreement is the functional equivalent of a corporation's bylaws and shareholders agreement.

PMB – Private mailbox rented from a small business, such as a UPS Store, Mr. Parcel, PostNet, etc. Note that a PMB is not a PO Box rented from the U.S. Postal Service.

PO BOX – A Post Office mail box rented from the U.S. Postal Service. Note that a PO Box is not a PMB.

REGISTERED AGENT – The person or entity designated to receive certain documents on behalf of your Texas limited liability company, including service of process if your LLC is sued. For privacy and other reasons, many LLC owners use a commercial registered agent service.

RETAIL PRODUCTS – Goods sold to members of the public as end users. These are not products that are sold to wholesalers for resale to others.

SOS – Acronym for Secretary of State. In this guide, it refers to the Texas Secretary of State.

SOS DIRECT – The name of the website where your business lawyer files your LLC's paperwork electronically with the Texas Secretary of State.

SALES TAX – A state tax paid by Texas customers who buy certain retail products from your LLC. The tax collected is then remitted by the LLC to the Texas Comptroller of Public Accounts.

TEXAS COMPTROLLER OF PUBLIC ACCOUNTS – The State of Texas revenue official that Texas LLCs deal with because of sales taxes and franchise taxes.

TEXAS SECRETARY OF STATE – The State of Texas government official whose office is responsible for processing formation and dissolution legal documents for Texas LLCs, corporations, and other business entities

Resources

Caution - just as technology changes quickly, so does the quality of service providers. What's a good resource today may become a poor or obsolete one tomorrow. In short, perform your own due diligence before using any of the following resources. Also note that each of these resources are listed in alphabetical order by topic, not by preference of the Author or Publisher of this guide.

Business Insurance

Jackie Torres Agency,
Nationwide Insurance
15635 Vision Dr Ste. 101
Pflugerville, TX 78660
512-252-1107
512-252-1201- fax
877-840-0419 - Toll free
torresj2@nationwide.com
http://www.nationwide.com/jackietorres
http://Iknowjackie.com

Internal Revenue Service
- Main website: http://irs.gov

- Apply for an *Employer Identification Number* (EIN) online: https://www.irs.gov/businesses/small-businesses-self-employed/apply-for-an-employer-identification-number-ein-online
- IRS Form W-9 download (PDF file): https://www.irs.gov/pub/irs-pdf/fw9.pdf
- *Disregarded Entity* Tax Treatment (default status for Single Member LLCs): If you have a single member LLC that has decided to be treated as a sole proprietorship by the IRS, you'll report income on the Schedule C that you attach to your annual IRS Form 1040 (PDF file) income tax return.
- Schedule C download (PDF file) - https://www.irs.gov/pub/irs-pdf/f1040sc.pdf
- IRS Form 1040 download (PDF file) - https://www.irs.gov/pub/irs-pdf/f1040.pdf
- *Partnership* Tax Return – IRS Form 1065. This form is used by multi-member LLCs that have decided to be treated as a partnership for tax purposes. Each member's income, etc. will be shown on an IRS Form K-1 (PDF file).
- IRS Form 1065 download(PDF file): https://www.irs.gov/pub/irs-pdf/f1065.pdf
- IRS Form K-1 download (PDF file): https://www.irs.gov/pub/irs-pdf/f1065sk1.pdf

- *Corporate* Entity Classification Election –
  IRS Form 8832 (PDF file). This form is used
  to elect to have your LLC treated by the IRS
  as a corporation for tax purposes. Note this
  election is optional. Most LLCs do not file it
  and are treated by default as either a sole
  proprietorship (single member LLC) or a
  partnership (multi-member LLC).
- IRS Form 8832 download (PDF file):
  http://www.irs.gov/pub/irs-pdf/f8832.pdf
- U.S. *Corporation* Income Tax Return – IRS
  Form 1120 (PDF file). If your LLC elects
  (using IRS Form 8832) to be treated as a
  corporation, the LLC will file a corporate
  income tax return.
- IRS Form 1120 download (PDF file):
  http://www.irs.gov/pub/irs-pdf/f1120.pdf

PayPal Business Services
- See
  https://www.paypal.com/us/webapps/mpp/merc
  hant

Registered Agent

Attorney Young and many of his clients use the following registered agent for their Texas limited liability companies. You may find others online by searching for "Texas registered agent" in the search engines.

Lone Star Registered Agent LLC
http://www.texasregisteredagents.com/
Tel: (972) 528-5960
700 Lavaca St.
Suite 1401
Austin, TX 78701

Texas Business Organizations Code
The state's business organizations code governs the formation, operation, and dissolution of Texas limited liability companies and other entities. You can find the code at this link.

Texas Comptroller of Public Accounts
- Business Resources:
  http://comptroller.texas.gov/business.php
- Sales Tax Permits:
  http://comptroller.texas.gov/taxpermit/
- Franchise Tax Reports:
  http://comptroller.texas.gov/taxinfo/franchise/

Texas Secretary of State

Corporations Section
P.O. Box 13697
Austin, TX 78711-3697
Tel: (512) 475-2755
Email: SOSDirect@sos.texas.gov

- SOSDirect: https://direct.sos.state.tx.us/
- Downloadable forms to print and file offline: http://www.sos.state.tx.us/corp/forms_boc.shtml
- Fee schedule: https://direct.sos.state.tx.us/help/help-corp.asp?pg=fee

U.S. Patent & Trademark Office
http://www.uspto.gov/

Disclosures And Disclaimers

Under no circumstances, including, but not limited to, negligence, shall the Author or the Publisher be liable for any special or consequential damages that result from the use of, or the inability to use this guide, even if the Author, the Publisher, or an authorized representative has been advised of the possibility of such damages. Applicable law may not allow the limitation or exclusion of liability or incidental or consequential damages, so the above limitation or exclusion may not apply to you. In no event shall the Author's or Publisher's total liability to you for all damages, losses, and causes of action (whether in contract, tort, including but not limited to, negligence or otherwise) exceed the amount paid by you, if any, for this guide.

You agree to hold the Author and the Publisher of this guide, principals, agents, affiliates, and employees harmless from any and all liability for all claims for damages due to injuries, including attorney fees and costs, incurred by you or caused to third parties by you, arising out of the products, services, and activities discussed in this guide, excepting only claims for gross negligence or intentional tort.

You agree that any and all claims for gross negligence or intentional tort shall be settled solely by confidential binding arbitration per the American Arbitration Association's commercial arbitration rules. All arbitration must occur in the municipality where the Author's principal place of business is located. Your claim cannot be aggregated with third party claims. Arbitration fees and costs shall be split equally, and you are solely responsible for your own lawyer fees.

Facts and information are believed to be accurate at the time they were placed in this guide. All data provided in this guide is to be used for information purposes only. The information contained within is not intended to provide specific legal, financial, tax, physical or mental health advice, or any other advice whatsoever, for any individual or company and should not be relied upon in that regard. The services described are only offered in jurisdictions where they may be legally offered. Information provided is not all-inclusive, and is limited to information that is made available and such information should not be relied upon as all-inclusive or accurate.

For more information about this policy, please contact the Author at the e-mail address listed in the Copyright Notice at the front of this guide.

IF YOU DO NOT AGREE WITH THESE TERMS AND EXPRESS CONDITIONS, DO NOT READ THIS GUIDE. YOUR USE OF THIS GUIDE, PRODUCTS, SERVICES, AND ANY PARTICIPATION IN ACTIVITIES MENTIONED IN THIS GUIDE, MEAN THAT YOU ARE AGREEING TO BE LEGALLY BOUND BY THESE TERMS.

Affiliate Compensation & Material Connections Disclosure

This guide may contain hyperlinks to websites and information created and maintained by other individuals and organizations. The Author and the Publisher do not control or guarantee the accuracy, completeness, relevance, or timeliness of any information or privacy policies posted on these linked websites.

You should assume that all references to products and services in this guide are made because material connections exist between the Author or Publisher and the providers of the mentioned products and services ("Provider"). You should also assume that all hyperlinks within this guide are affiliate links for (a) the Author, (b) the Publisher, or (c) someone else who is an affiliate for the mentioned products and services (individually and collectively, the "Affiliate").

The Affiliate recommends products and services in this guide based in part on a good faith belief that the purchase of such products or services will help readers in general.

The Affiliate has this good faith belief because (a) the Affiliate has tried the product or service mentioned prior to recommending it or (b) the Affiliate has researched the reputation of the Provider and has made the decision to recommend the Provider's products or services based on the Provider's history of providing these or other products or services.

The representations made by the Affiliate about products and services reflect the Affiliate's honest opinion based upon the facts known to the Affiliate at the time this guide was published.

Because there is a material connection between the Affiliate and Providers of products or services mentioned in this guide, you should always assume that the Affiliate may be biased because of the Affiliate's relationship with a Provider and/or because the Affiliate has received or will receive something of value from a Provider.

Perform your own due diligence before purchasing a product or service mentioned in this guide.

The type of compensation received by the Affiliate may vary. In some instances, the Affiliate may receive complimentary products (such as a review copy), services, or money from a Provider prior to mentioning the Provider's products or services in this guide.

In addition, the Affiliate may receive a monetary commission or non-monetary compensation when you take action by clicking on a hyperlink in this guide. This includes, but is not limited to, when you purchase a product or service from a Provider after clicking on an affiliate link in this guide.

Purchase Price

Although the Publisher believes the price is fair for the value that you receive, you understand and agree that the purchase price for this guide has been arbitrarily set by the Publisher or the vendor who sold you this guide. This price bears no relationship to objective standards.

Due Diligence

You are advised to do your own due diligence when it comes to making any decisions. Use caution and seek the advice of qualified professionals before acting upon the contents of this guide or any other information. You shall not consider any examples, documents, or other content in this guide or otherwise provided by the Author or Publisher to be the equivalent of professional advice.

The Author and the Publisher assume no responsibility for any losses or damages resulting from your use of any link, information, or opportunity contained in this guide or within any other information disclosed by the Author or the Publisher in any form whatsoever.

YOU SHOULD ALWAYS CONDUCT YOUR OWN INVESTIGATION (PERFORM DUE DILIGENCE) BEFORE BUYING PRODUCTS OR SERVICES FROM ANYONE OFFLINE OR VIA THE INTERNET. THIS INCLUDES PRODUCTS AND SERVICES SOLD VIA HYPERLINKS CONTAINED IN THIS GUIDE.